IMPORTA... **license and refer t**... **s before keeping a**...

WHERE TO FISH: Inland/Near Shore

Piers

- Most piers are well maintained, and a few are lighted and have restrooms; piers may even sell bait and tackle. Most are barebones affairs, and you'll need to bring all your gear and bait with you.

- Some piers may charge a small daily fee to fish. Laws vary, but on most piers you'll need a saltwater fishing license.

- For more success, watch for when and where locals go fishing. In some seasons, night fishing might be best.

- As for gear and bait, take note of the water habitat of the pier. If it's over a rocky shore, rig your gear for fish that feed on barnacles and crabs. If it's built atop sand, use a surf rig. And don't forget to try your luck under the pier; some fish take shelter right around the pier pilings.

Surf

- Before you hit the beach, visit a bait shop for advice.

- When surf fishing, any rod will work, as long as it can handle a 2–4 oz. sinker.

- Large 10–15 foot-long rods are used when long casts are needed to reach fish, but fish often feed just at the beach line.

- Even small surf fish are strong, so anchor your rod well. (Don't try to use a cooler, or you might lose your gear.)

- Most surf fish have sharp teeth, so attach a strong leader below the weight. Use a short one when in rough surf and a long one when waves are smaller. You want enough weight in your leader so it doesn't roll down the beach, but it needs to be light enough to roll in the surf.

- An outgoing tide is commonly thought to be the best fishing, but on beaches with a deep ledge, an incoming tide is often better. Wherever you're fishing, fishing with a tidal current is better than with a slack tide.

- Bring pliers and gloves. Some fish have sharp teeth!

Red Drum

Surf, shell bars and weedy flats

Dark spot at base of
tail above lateral
line; snout
protrudes
beyond lower lip

14–20"
3–8 lb.

SALTWATER • BRACKISH

Black Drum

*Bays, estuaries
and channels*

4–5 wide vertical
bars; horizontal
mouth with
many chin barbels

20–24"
15–20 lb.

SALTWATER • BRACKISH

Freshwater Drum

Lakes and slow streams

Lateral line runs
from head
through tail

10–12"
2–5 lb.

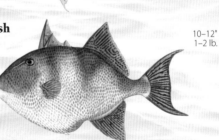

FRESHWATER

Gray Triggerfish

Rocks and reefs

Leathery skin;
the first dorsal
spine can
lock into a
vertical position

10–12"
1–2 lb.

SALTWATER

Blackfish (Tautog)

*Inshore around jetties,
rocks and piers*

Big lips; no scales
on gill covers

15–20"
2–4 lb.

SALTWATER

AVERAGE CATCH
(see note on page 3)

Southern Kingfish
Surf to deeper water

Single barbel
under chin;
upper tail
lobe short and
slightly pointed

SALTWATER

9–12"
¾–1 lb.

Spotted Sea Trout
Grass and shell flats

Dark spots over
body and
fins; inside of
mouth orange

SALTWATER

12–15"
2–3 lb.

Weakfish
Deep channels and bays

Diagonal lines of
small spots

SALTWATER

18–24"
3–5 lb.

Mutton Snapper
*Over rocks in bays
and estuaries*

Eye-sized black
spot centered
above midline

SALTWATER

18–24"
5–15 lb.

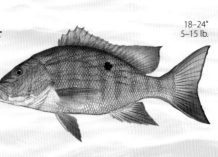

AVERAGE CATCH
(see note on page 3)

Needlefish

*Most shallow water areas
connected to saltwater*

Lower jaw
longer than
upper jaw

10–12"
8–16 oz.

SALTWATER • BRACKISH • FRESHWATER

Puffers

Near rocks and reefs

Sloping forehead
with crescent-
shaped marks
under eyes

6–10"
8–12 oz.

SALTWATER • BRACKISH

Summer Flounder

*Shallow water with
soft bottom*

Spots with faint or no
"eye" ring

16–22"
3–5 lb.

SALTWATER • BRACKISH

Spadefish

Rocks and reefs

3–6 dark bands;
rear dorsal
fin matches
anal fin

8–12"
1–2 lb.

SALTWATER

AVERAGE CATCH
(see note on page 3)

Flathead Catfish

Deep lakes and rivers

Broad, flattened head with a pronounced underbite

20–28"
15–20 lb.

FRESHWATER

Bullheads

Shallow water of lakes and slow streams

Rounded tail and a pronounced overbite

9–10"
¾–1 lb.

FRESHWATER

Bowfin

Weedy lakes and streams

Continuous dorsal fin; bony plates covering head

12–14"
3–4 lb.

FRESHWATER

Longnose Gar

Quiet waters of larger rivers and lakes

Long, thin snout; long, narrow body

18–24"
3–5 lb.

FRESHWATER • BRACKISH

Atlantic Croaker

Sand or shell bottom, in surf or near piers

Small barbels under jaw

8–12"
1–1½ lb.

SALTWATER • BRACKISH

AVERAGE CATCH
(see note on page 3)

Bluefish

Surf and channels

Large mouth with
sharp teeth;
anal fin same
shape as rear
dorsal fin

8–10"
1–2 lb.

SALTWATER

Great Barracuda

Shallow reefs and grass flats

Dark blotches
on lower
sides; large,
sharp teeth

18–24"
5–10 lb.

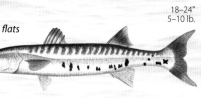

SALTWATER

Striped Bass

*Reefs, surf and large rivers
and lakes*

7-8 unbroken
stripes; two
tooth patches
on tongue

18–24"
5–20 lb.

SALTWATER • BRACKISH • FRESH

Spot

*Surf, shallow bays
and estuaries*

Dark spot behind
gill above
pectoral fin

6–8"
⅓–¾ lb.

SALTWATER • BRACKISH

Striped Mullet

Shallow coastal waters

Large mouth
with sharp
teeth; anal fin
same shape as
rear dorsal fin

10–12"
1–2 lb.

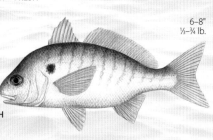

SALTWATER • BRACKISH •
FRESHWATER

Pinfish

Shallow water with structure

Dark spot on lateral line above pectoral fins

3–6"
4–8 oz.

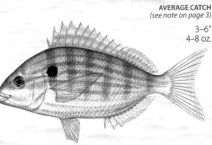

SALTWATER

Pigfish

Shallow coastal waters over a mud bottom

Many bronze bars on upper body; small mouth with thin lips

4–8"
1–2 lb.

SALTWATER • BRACKISH

Porgies (Whitebone Porgy)

Shallow water with structure out to about 100'

Steeply sloped from snout to dorsal fin; eyes high on head

6–18"
½–4 lb.

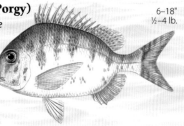

SALTWATER

White Catfish

Shallow, still water with good cover

White chin barbels; 19–23 rays in anal fin

10–12"
1–2 lb.

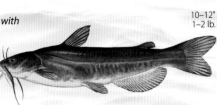

FRESHWATER

Hardhead Catfish

Water with high turbidity and low salinity

Locking venomous spines in dorsal and pectoral fins

5–8"
6–8 oz.

SALTWATER • BRACKISH

9

AVERAGE CATCH
(see note on page 3)

Largemouth Bass

Most lakes and rivers

Mouth extends
well beyond eye

FRESHWATER •
BRACKISH

10–12"
1–3 lb.

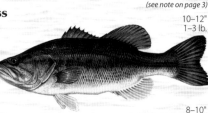

Spotted Bass

*Streams and large
impoundments*

Diamond-shaped
blotches form
dark stripe on side

FRESHWATER

8–10"
1–2 lb.

White Crappie

*Deeper lakes with
open water*

Only sunfish with
six spines in the
dorsal and
anal fins

FRESHWATER

6–8"
8–12 oz.

Shellcracker

*Lakes and streams
with cover*

Dark gill spot
with a red margin

FRESHWATER •
BRACKISH

6–8"
8–16 oz.

Bluegill

*Lakes and streams
with cover*

Large dark gill
spot with a
dark margin

FRESHWATER

4–6"
5–8 oz.

Carolina Pompano

Surf over sandy bottom

Deep, flat body;
blunt nose with
small mouth;
yellowish tail

SALTWATER

10–12"
1–2 lb.

Sheepshead

*Shallow bays, estuaries
and coastal streams*

5–7 dark bands;
black fins; flat
protruding teeth

SALTWATER •
BRACKISH

8–12"
2–3 lb.

Tarpon

*Shallow bays, estuaries and
coastal streams*

Large plate-like
scales; last ray
of dorsal fin
very long

SALTWATER • BRACKISH • FRESHWATER

3–4'
30–50 lb.

American Shad

*Open ocean; spawns in
freshwater streams*

Black spot behind
and just above
gill cover

SALTWATER • BRACKISH • FRESHWATER

12–20"
1–3 lb.

Lookdown

*Shallow water with
a hard bottom*

Forehead and
face are sharply
slanted

SALTWATER

6–10"
8–12 oz.

11

AVERAGE CATCH
(see note on page 3)

Grunts

Shallow, rocky nearshore waters

Small baitfish that makes a grunting sound when stressed

SALTWATER

3–5"
4–6 oz.

Gafftopsail Catfish

Shallow, still coastal waters

Four mouth barbels; upper ones reach anal fins; pectoral and dorsal fin ends in a long filament

SALTWATER

15–20"
2–3 lb.

Channel Catfish

Clean lakes and streams

Anal fin is spotted and has 24–30 rays

FRESHWATER

15–20"
2–4 lb.

Pickerel

Freshwater lakes and rivers

Torpedo-shaped body; dark bar under the eye

FRESHWATER

18–24"
1–3 lb.

Common Carp

Soft-bottomed lakes and streams

Sucker mouth has two barbels

FRESHWATER

18–20"
2–12 lb.

AVERAGE CATCH
(see note on page 3)

Crevalle Jack

Bays, estuaries and coastal rivers

Dark spot on gill cover and pectoral fin

SALTWATER • BRACKISH

18–24"
10–20 lb.

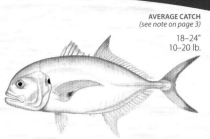

Bonnethead

Salty estuaries and bays

Spade-shaped head; tall dorsal fin

SALTWATER

24–36"
3–5 lb.

Bull Shark

Bays, estuaries and freshwater

Stout body; rounded snout

SALTWATER •
BRACKISH • FRESHWATER

6–7'
100–150 lb.

Sturgeon

Clear streams out to deep ocean

Plate-like scales, rounded snout

SALTWATER • BRACKISH • FRESHWATER

3–7'
50–400 lb.

AVERAGE CATCH
(see note on page 3)

American Eel

Estuaries and freshwater streams

Dorsal fin starts
well behind
pectoral fin

SALTWATER • BRACKISH •
FRESHWATER

20–30"
2–4 lb.

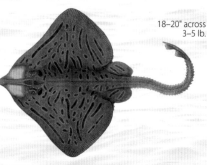

Clearnose Skate

*Shallow waters
with a soft bottom*

Pointed snout
with two clear
spots; no
stinger on tail

SALTWATER

18–20" across
3–5 lb.

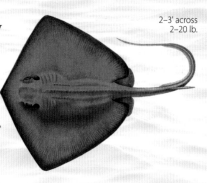

Southern Stingray

*Shallow bays
and estuaries*

Midline thorns
from eyes to tail;
whip-like tail with
a stinger

SALTWATER • BRACKISH •
FRESHWATER

2–3' across
2–20 lb.

IMPORTANT NOTE: Always obtain a fishing license and refer to area fishing regulations/slot limits before keeping any fish.

WHERE TO FISH: Deepwater/Offshore

Group Fishing Launches

• These boats take anywhere from a few people to as many as 50 people at one time on fishing trips; reservations are a good idea.

• Bait, tackle and fishing advice are provided, but you often have to bring your own drinks/lunch; larger vessels offer concessions. Most launches offer bathrooms, although they can be very small.

• If you're worried about getting seasick, keep in mind that the large vessels are more stable than smaller ones. If concerned, consider taking a seasickness-prevention pill an hour before you leave, and one as you get on board.

• When selecting a launch boat, ask about the ride to the fishing grounds. In some areas the ride out to the reefs is a couple hours long, and this can considerably shorten your fishing day.

• If possible, stop by the landing dock a few afternoons before you go out and see what the boat is bringing in.

• Once you're on the water, the crews are very helpful, and there is frequently a tip pail passed before you land. On smaller boats, the captain and the mate do all they can to help you catch fish; on bigger boats you are more on your own.

Charter Boats

• When you're new to an area, the surest way to catch fish is also the most expensive: hiring a charter boat and a guide just for your fishing party. Most marinas and bait shops along the coast can put you in contact with charter services. Charters provide all the equipment you'll need, and sometimes lunch.

Rent a Boat

• If you have your own fishing tackle and boating experience, rent a boat at an area marina. Sometimes you have the option of hiring a first mate to guide you to good fishing areas.

• You'll need a fishing license, and you'll need to provide your own bait, but you'll get to be on your own. Be warned that you should know the area, keep an eye on the weather, understand buoys and markers, and have very good navigation tools. Obviously, taking off on your own can be dangerous if you're unprepared.

AVERAGE CATCH
(see note on page 15)

Tripletail

*Open water
near floating objects*

Rear dorsal and
anal fin are set
far back and
rounded like
the tail fin

SALTWATER

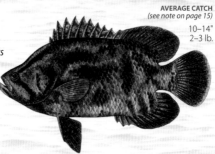

10–14"
2–3 lb.

Black Sea Bass

*Open water near
shallow reefs*

Scales have
pale centers
that form
faint stripes

SALTWATER

8–10"
1–2 lb.

Red Snapper

Deep reefs

Deep body
with red fins;
pointed anal fin

SALTWATER

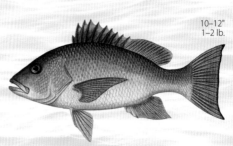

10–12"
1–2 lb.

Red Grouper

*Shallow to deep
rock walls*

Scattered white
spots over pale
blotches; inside
of mouth is red
or orange

SALTWATER

12–15"
5–10 lb.

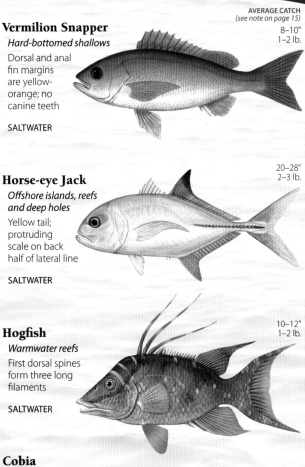

Vermilion Snapper

Hard-bottomed shallows

Dorsal and anal
fin margins
are yellow-
orange; no
canine teeth

8–10"
1–2 lb.

SALTWATER

Horse-eye Jack

*Offshore islands, reefs
and deep holes*

Yellow tail;
protruding
scale on back
half of lateral line

20–28"
2–3 lb.

SALTWATER

Hogfish

Warmwater reefs

First dorsal spines
form three long
filaments

10–12"
1–2 lb.

SALTWATER

Cobia

*Open water around platforms,
wrecks and buoys*

Flattened head with
a protruding
lower lip; dark
stripe from
eye to tail

2–3'
10–20 lb.

SALTWATER

AVERAGE CATCH
(see note on page 15)

Spanish Mackerel

Open water of bays and estuaries

Starting at the dorsal fin, the lateral line curves evenly to tail

16–20"
1–2 lb.

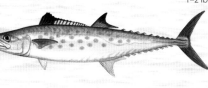

SALTWATER

Wahoo

Deep water at current changes

Vivid blue and white stripes; elongated mouth

24–30"
20–50 lb.

SALTWATER

Dorado

Surface water of the open Atlantic

Deep head tapering to tail; dorsal fin runs from head to tail

20–26"
5–15 lb.

SALTWATER

Bonito

Open, deep water, often close to shore

4–5 dark spots below pectoral fins; dark wavy bars above lateral line

12–14"
3–4 lb.

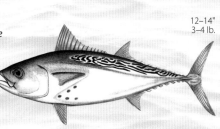

SALTWATER

Ballyhoo

Open water over reefs and rocks

Long lower jaw protrudes and forms a beak; large eye

10–15"
9–16 oz.

SALTWATER

AVERAGE CATCH
(see note on page 15)

Greater Amberjack

Offshore near deep structures

Dark olive band from mouth through eye to dorsal fin

SALTWATER

3–4'
10–20 lb.

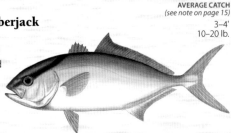

Blackfin Tuna

Open offshore water

All finlets dusky gray or black with white tips

SALTWATER

2–3'
5–15 lb.

Sailfish

Open water near reefs and breaks

Large deep dorsal fin is 150% of body depth

SALTWATER

4–7'
20–40 lb.

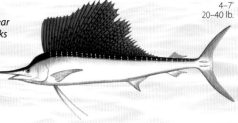

White Marlin

Deep offshore waters

Round tips on dorsal, anal and pectoral fins

SALTWATER

3–5'
50–100 lb.

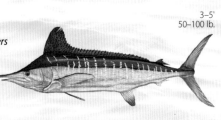

Blacktip Shark

Open bays and offshore waters

Black tips on all fins

SALTWATER

3–5'
5–25 lb.

Fighting Ability

Some people fish to eat, whereas others enjoy the fight of reeling a fish in. This chart provides an unofficial ranking of how hard each fish species fights. Perhaps surprisingly, not all especially sought-after fish are strong fighters.

Strong

Bonnethead	Dorado	Sheepshead
Blackfin Tuna	Flathead Catfish	Shellcracker
Blacktip Shark	Gray Triggerfish	Spadefish
Bluefish	Great Barracuda*	Spotted Bass
Bluegill*	Greater Amberjack	Striped Bass*
Bonito	Hogfish	Sturgeon
Bowfin	Horse-eye Jack	Summer Flounder*
Bull Shark	Largemouth Bass*	Tarpon*
Cobia	Longnose Gar	Vermilion Snapper
Common Carp	Red Drum	Wahoo
Crevalle Jack	Sailfish*	White Marlin*

Average

American Eel	Gafftopsail Catfish	Southern Kingfish
Black Drum*	Lookdown	Southern Stingray
Blackfish	Mutton Snapper	Striped Mullet
Black Sea Bass	Pickerel	Tripletail
Carolina Pompano*	Pigfish	White Catfish
Channel Catfish*	Porgies	White Crappie*
Clearnose Skate	Red Snapper*	
Freshwater Drum	Red Grouper	

Poor

American Shad	Hardhead Catfish	Spanish Mackerel
Atlantic Croaker	Needlefish	Spotted Sea Trout*
Bullheads	Pinfish	Spot
Ballyhoo	Puffer	Weakfish*
Grunts		

* *denotes popular game fish*

Table Quality

If you're fishing and looking to cook your catch, the following chart outlines some of the most popular fish for the table.

Excellent

American Eel	Gray Triggerfish	Spadefish
Blackfin Tuna*	Hogfish	Striped Bass*
Black Sea Bass	Lookdown	Summer Flounder*
Bluegill*	Red Drum*	Vermilion Snapper
Carolina Pompano*	Red Grouper	Wahoo
Cobia	Red Snapper*	White Crappie*
Channel Catfish*	Sailfish*	
Dorado	Shellcracker	

Average

Atlantic Croaker	Pickerel	Spotted Sea Trout*
Black Drum*	Pigfish	Spot
Blackfish	Porgies	Striped Mullet
Flathead Catfish	Sheepshead	Tripletail
Grunts	Southern Kingfish	Weakfish*
Largemouth Bass*	Spanish Mackerel	White Catfish
Mutton Snapper	Spotted Bass	

Eaten by a Few

Bonnethead	Bull Shark	Greater Amberjack
Bluefish	Common Carp	Horse-eye Jack
Bonito	Crevalle Jack	Freshwater Drum
Bowfin	Gafftopsail Catfish	Sturgeon
Bullhead	Great Barracuda*	

Not Often Eaten

American Shad	Longnose Gar	Southern Stingray
Ballyhoo	Needlefish	White Marlin*
Blacktip Shark	Pinfish	Tarpon*
Clearnose Skate	Puffers	
Hardhead Catfish	**(potentially toxic)**	

* *denotes popular game fish*

Adventure Quick Guides

Includes Saltwater and Freshwater Fish

Your guide to 67 of the most popular sport fish of the inland waters, surf and deepwater

- Includes sport fish from freshwater, brackish water and saltwater

- Organized by where you're fishing, whether inland, close to shore or deep sea fishing

- Pocket-sized format—easier than laminated foldouts

- Waterproof and tear-resistant durability

- Professional illustrations that show key markings

Get all the Adventure Quick Guides for the Southeast

$9.95

Adventure
PUBLICATIONS

Adventure Publications
820 Cleveland Street South
Cambridge, Minnesota 55008
(800) 678-7006
www.adventurepublications.net
NATURE/FISH/ATLANTIC COAST

ISBN 978-1-59193-701-2

5 0 9 9 5

9 781591 937012